December Holidays

bowmar

written by Lucille Wood
designed and illustrated by Paul Taylor

RHYTHMS TO READING
Book and Record Sets
A Multi-Sensory Approach to Music and Reading

A companion recording is available for this book and all others in the RHYTHMS TO READING series. Each picture in this book represents an action song or a descriptive musical composition which is included on the long-playing record.

The simple text under each picture provides a unique, multi-sensory experience for the young child. He reads about the activities to which he has just responded in movement and song. This text is also included on the recording for classroom use or at the listening post.

On the left-hand page, beginning on page 4, are printed the full story and song lyrics heard on the recording. This page is for the use of teachers, parents and children who have had reading experience.

Repetition is essential to learning. Learning which might otherwise be derived from tedious drill is here developed in an enjoyable, esthetic context.

Research indicates that children learn to read more quickly and easily words that are related to large muscle activity, esthetic experience and tongue-tickling rhymes.

When reading experiences are introduced through music, song and vigorous movement

- *memory is reinforced and tensions released, creating an atmosphere that encourages learning.*
- *the flow of language comes more naturally, encouraging the child to read in complete sentences.*
- *the number of clues which aid the child in reading are multiplied.*
- *word meanings are clarified and sight vocabulary is developed automatically.*

First Printing .... January 1971
Second Printing .... March 1972

December is a happy time.

December is a happy time, a time for music.
"Jingle Bells" is one of our favorite songs.
We play jingle bells as we sing.
Sometimes we are the high stepping horses
that pull the sleigh.

Dashing through the snow in a one-horse open sleigh,
O'er the fields we go, laughing all the way;
Bells on bobtail ring, making spirits bright,
What fun it is to ride and sing a sleighing song tonight.

Jingle bells, jingle bells, jingle all the way
Oh, what fun it is to ride in a one-horse open sleigh!
Jingle bells, jingle bells, jingle all the way,
Oh what fun it is to ride in a one-horse open sleigh!

Day or two ago I thought I'd take a ride,
And soon Miss Fanny Bright was seated by my side;
The horse was lean and lank, misfortune seemed his lot;
He got into a drifted bank and we, we got upsot.

Jingle bells, jingle bells, jingle all the way
Oh, what fun it is to ride in a one-horse open sleigh!
Jingle bells, jingle bells, jingle all the way,
Oh what fun it is to ride in a one-horse open sleigh!

We sing "Jingle Bells" and trot like horses.

We sing a dreidel song for the Hanukkah holidays.
We take turns playing the finger cymbals
or tambourines as we sing.

I have a little dreidel,
A pretty little top;
Around and 'round it's spinning,
I'll never let it stop!
Oh, dreidel, dreidel, dreidel,
Oh, little top that spins
The children all are happy,
When Hanukkah begins!
(Repeat)

We sing a dreidel song for Hanukkah.

We spin around
and fall down like the dreidel in this song.

We are the dreidels of Hanukkah,
Spin all around, spin all around,
We are the dreidels of Hanukkah,
Spin all around, spin all around.
Spin and spin and spin and spin;
Fall to the ground, fall to the ground.
(Repeat)

(Trudi Behar)

We spin around and fall down like the dreidel.

In this song, nine of us are candles of the menorah.
One is the large shamash candle
from which the other candles are lighted.

(1) Mister Shamash, light one candle,
Mister Shamash, burn it bright.
Flicker, flicker, one burning candle,
Hanukkah is here.
Flicker, flicker, one burning candle,
Hanukkah is here.

(2) Mister Shamash, light one candle
Mister Shamash, burn it bright.
Flicker, flicker, two burning candles
Hanukkah is here.
Flicker, flicker, two burning candles
Hanukkah is here.

(3) Three burning candles, etc.

(4) Four burning candles, etc.

(5) Five burning candles, etc.

(6) Six burning candles, etc.

(7) Seven burning candles, etc.

(8) Eight burning candles, etc.

(Miriam Behar)

We are the nine candles of the menorah.

On December holidays we play with new toys.
Let's have a toy parade.
Which toy will you be?

We march in a toy parade.

Let's decorate a Christmas tree:
Reach down to the floor to get a sparkling decoration,
pick it up and fasten it on the branch of a tree.

We put a shining star on the Christmas tree.

After the tree is decorated,
we walk around it to the music of a music box
which runs down and finally stops.
It plays a Christmas tree song
from a faraway country.

We walk around the Christmas tree.

We sing a song about Santa Claus and his toys.

Up on the housetop, reindeer pause,
Out jumps good old Santa Claus;
Down through the chimney with lots of toys,
All for the little ones, Christmas joys.

Ho! Ho! Ho! Who wouldn't go,
Ho! Ho! Ho! Who wouldn't go
Up on the housetop, Click! Click! Click!
Down through the chimney with good Saint Nick.
(Repeat)

We sing about Santa Claus and his toys.

We have a turn trotting like the eight reindeer pulling Santa Claus in his sleigh.

We trot like eight reindeer pulling Santa's sleigh.

We play a Christmas game.
While sitting in a circle and singing,
we pass around a hat or a penny.
The boy or girl who has the hat or penny
at the end of the song is the old man
who must sit in the center of the circle.
When there are five old men
sitting in the center of the circle,
the game is over.

Christmas is coming, the goose is getting fat,
Please to put a penny in an old man's hat;
If you haven't got a penny then a ha'penny will do,
If you haven't got a ha'penny, God bless you.
(Repeat four times)

We play a Christmas game with an old man's hat.

With a blindfold over our eyes,
we take turns swinging a big stick
at a brightly colored piñata.
When the piñata is broken, candy falls out.

Andale, niño, no pierdas el tino,
Que de la distancia se pierde el camino,
Con los ojos bien vendados,
En las manos un bastón,
Ya se rompe la piñata sin tenerle compasión.

¡Dale, dale, dale! No pierdas el tino,
Que de la distancia se pierde el camino.
¡Dale, dale, dale! No pierdas el tino,
Que de la distancia se pierde el camino.

We swing a big stick and break the piñata.

We play the Christmas story
about Mary and Joseph and the Baby in a manger.

Wind through the olive trees,
Softly did blow.
Round little Bethlehem,
Long, long ago.

Sheep on the hillside lay,
Whiter than snow.
Shepherds were watching them,
Long, long ago.

Then from the starry skies,
Angels bent low.
Singing their songs of joy,
Long, long ago.

Wise men were following
A star that did glow.
Far over Bethlehem,
Long, long ago.

We play the Christmas story.

Shepherds and Wise Men and Angels
bring their gifts or songs
to the baby Jesus.

We bring our gifts to the Baby in the manger.